The Greening

GARDEN
THOUGHTS
WITH
CELTIC
PRAYERS

The Greening

GARDEN THOUGHTS WITH CELTIC PRAYERS

Lucinda Avery

ANAMCHARA BOOKS

Copyright © Anamchara Books, 2020.
All rights reserved.

ANAMCHARA BOOKS
Vestal, New York 13850
www.AnamcharaBooks.com

IngramSpark Paperback ISBN:
978-1-62524-785-8

Cover design, interior layout, and illustrations
by Micaela Grace.

CONTENTS

Introduction	9
1. The Beauty of a Garden	13
2. Joy in the Garden	21
3. The Creativity of a Garden	33
4. Lessons of the Garden	41
5. The Humility, Patience, & Faith of Gardening	51
6. Healing in the Garden	65
7. The Miracle of Gardening	75
8. Humans & Nature in the Garden	89
9. Time & the Garden	101
10. God in the Garden	111
11. We Are the Garden	129
About the Sources	139

And the Life-Giver planted
a garden in the east of Eden.

—GENESIS 2

What was Paradise but a garden,
an orchard of trees
and herbs, full of pleasure,
and nothing there but delight.

—WILLIAM LAWSON

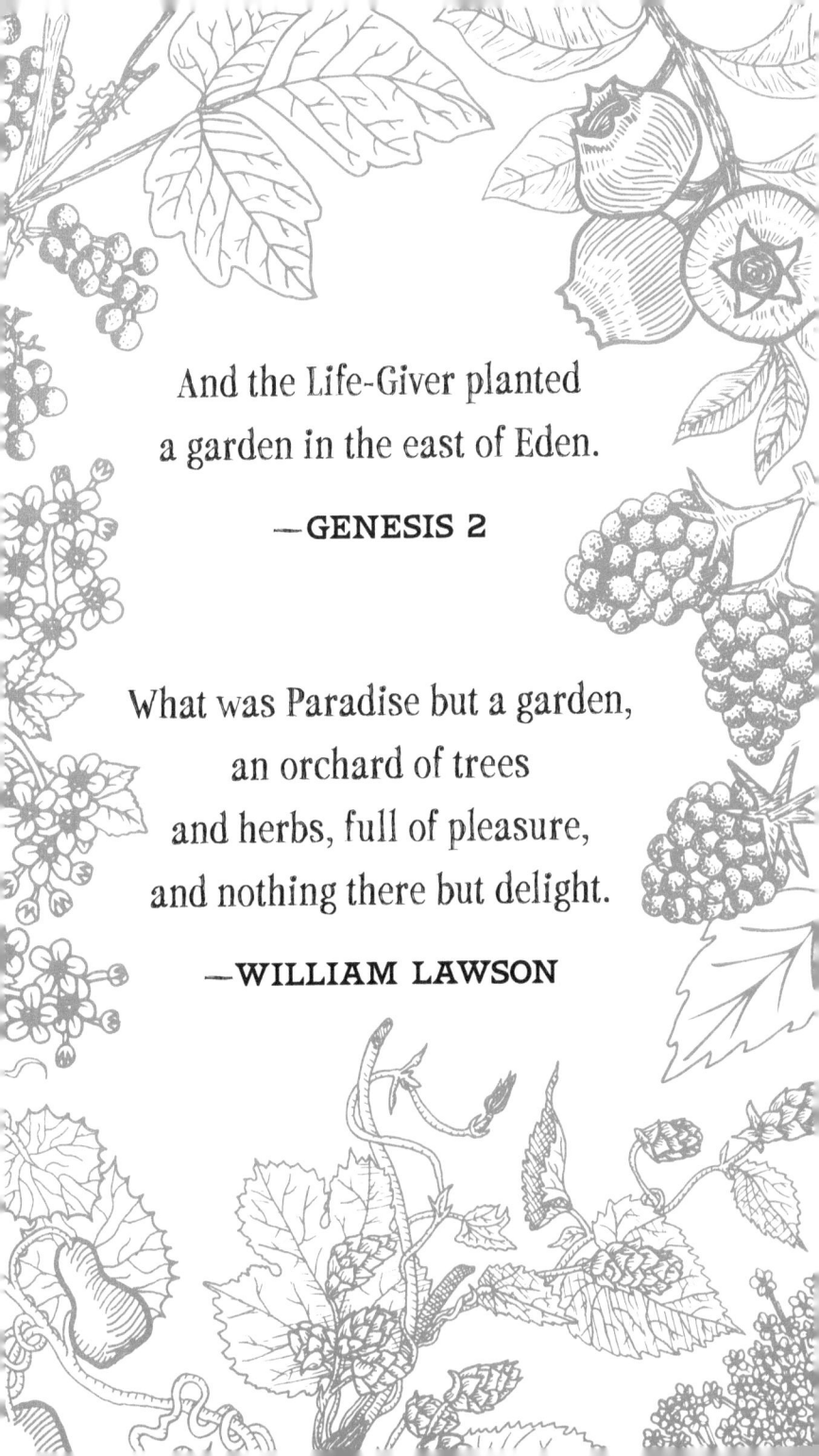

INTRODUCTION

I am in love with the green earth.

—CHARLES LAMB

Green fingers are the
extension of a verdant heart.

—FLANNERY O'CONNOR

In the eleventh century, Hildegard von Bingen wrote about *viriditas*, the "greening force" that is at work throughout the world. She used the word to describe the power of plants to put forth leaves and fruit, but she also saw the same force in human beings' ability to grow and heal—and to be co-creators with the Divine.

In Hildegard's garden, she saw the Divine nature—freshness, fruitfulness, vitality, growth. These, she believed, are the essential characteristics of God, and she learned about them from her garden.

I too have learned much about physical and spiritual health from my garden. For me, my garden, my being, and God are so interwoven that it is difficult for me to see where one begins and the other leaves off. My garden constantly reminds me of our deep connection with the life force that sustains the cosmos and also every living thing.

The book that follows contains "green thoughts" from other writers, words I have collected over the years that speak to me about my love of gardens. I have also included here some of my own garden meditations, which are based on prayers from the *Carmina Gadelica*, the collection of Celtic prayers created by Alexander Carmichael at the very beginning of the twentieth century. Whether you garden yourself, or only enjoy looking at gardens, I hope these thoughts speak to you as much as they have to me.

"There is a power that has been since all eternity, and that force and potentiality is green!"

wrote Hildegard. May you too experience in your own life the rich and vital power of soil and seed, leaf and branch, flower and fruit.

—Lucinda Avery

To forget how to dig the earth and
to tend the soil is to forget ourselves.

—MAHATMA GANDHI

Let us celebrate the soil.

—CHARLES DUDLEY WARNER

1

THE BEAUTY OF A GARDEN

There is material enough in
a single flower for
the ornament of
a score of cathedrals.

—JOHN RUSKIN

Here in my garden,
I bend my knee
to the beauty I see beneath me,
to the beauty I see above me,
to the beauty I see all around me.
O Great Being, Spirit of Beauty,
bestow on me eyes to see
beauty in leaf, beauty in flower,
beauty in love, beauty in power,
beauty in stem, beauty in fruit,
beauty in soil, beauty in root.
Beauty on earth as it is in heaven,
here in my garden,
in shade and light, by day and night,
I bend my knee to beauty.

That we find . . . a poppy beautiful
means that we are less alone,
that we are more deeply inserted
into existence than the course
of a single life would lead us to believe.

—JOHN BERGER

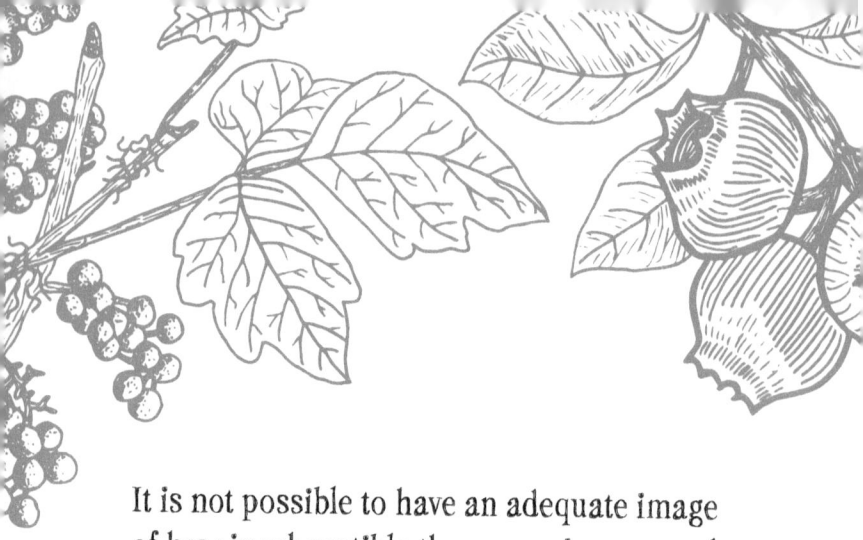

It is not possible to have an adequate image of how inexhaustible the expansiveness and possibilities of life are. No fate, no rejection, no hardship is entirely without prospects; somewhere the densest shrub can yield leaves, a flower, a fruit. . . . And if this fruit is bitter, it will have astonished at least one eye, and will have provided it pleasure. . . . And if the fruit were to fall, it would fall into the abundance of that which is yet to come. Even in its final decay it contributes to this future by turning it into more abundant, more colorful, and more urgent growth.

—RAINER MARIA RILKE

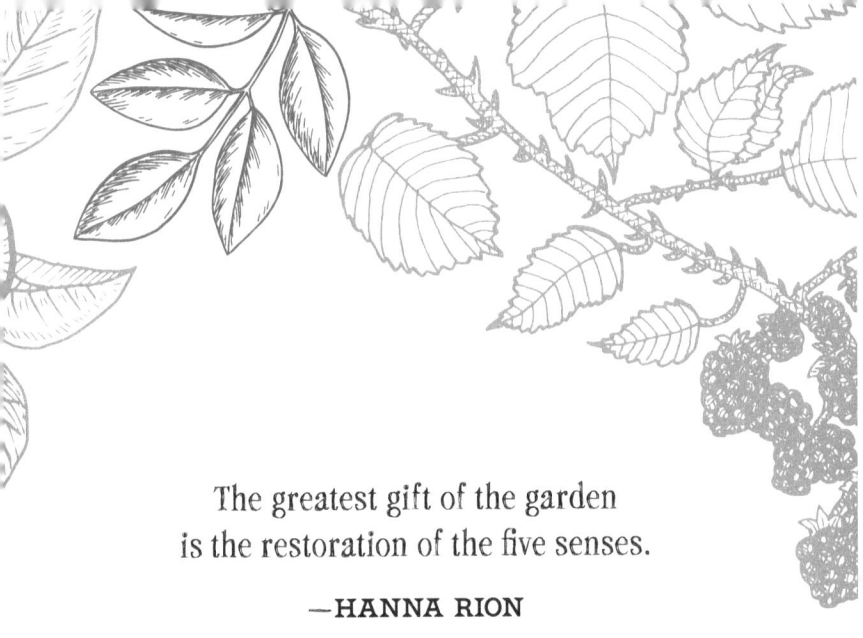

The greatest gift of the garden
is the restoration of the five senses.

—HANNA RION

Flowers whisper "Beauty!" to the world,
even as they fade, wilt, fall.

—DR. SUNWOLF

Flowers don't worry
about how they're going to bloom.
They just open up and turn toward the light
and that makes them beautiful.

—JIM CARREY

> There is simply the rose;
> it is perfect in every moment of its existence.
>
> —RALPH WALDO EMERSON

No Paradise? Have you no eyes, no ears? Have you not seen flowers growing, heard birds singing? Have you no heart to feel these things? ... Do you not realize that these beauties are shouting aloud the promise of the joy to come? ... They shout so loud about it that one might almost say they are the joy to come. Paradise is already present in this world, even as March daffodils dancing in the wind are present in the green shoots of February.

—ELIZABETH GOUDGE

Beauty with me lying down,
beauty with me rising up,
beauty with me in each ray of light.
Not a single blade of grass,
not a single petal or leaf,
but brims with beauty.
All Earth is my garden,
brimming with beauty.
Beauty with me sleeping,
beauty with me waking,
not one day without beauty.
Spirit of Beauty, clear my sight
to see You, even hidden.
Turn city streets
into Your garden bright.
Show me Your beauty
wherever I turn.

THE BEAUTY OF A GARDEN

2
JOY IN THE GARDEN

The one who plants
a garden
plants happiness.

—CHINESE PROVERB

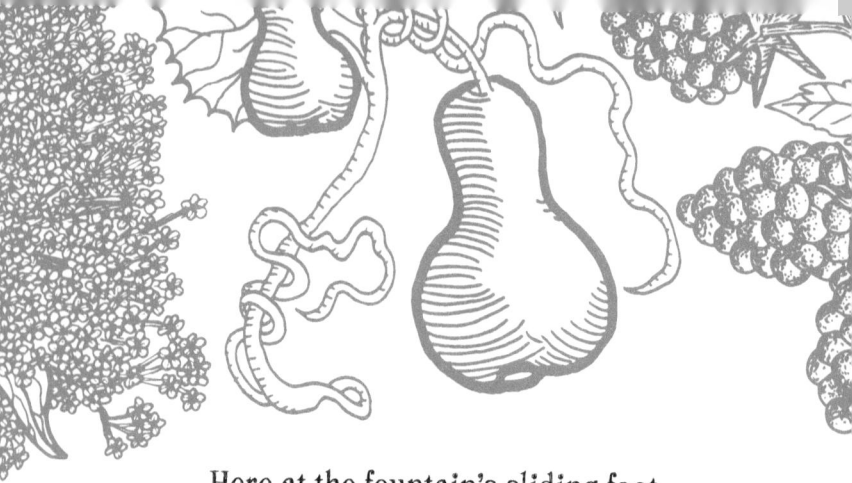

Here at the fountain's sliding foot,
Or at some fruit-tree's mossy root,
Casting the body's vest aside,
My soul into the boughs doth glide;
There, like a bird, it sits and sings,
Then whets and combs its silver wings,
And, till prepared for longer flight,
Waves in its plumes the various light.
Such was that happy Garden-state. . . .

—ANDREW MARVEL

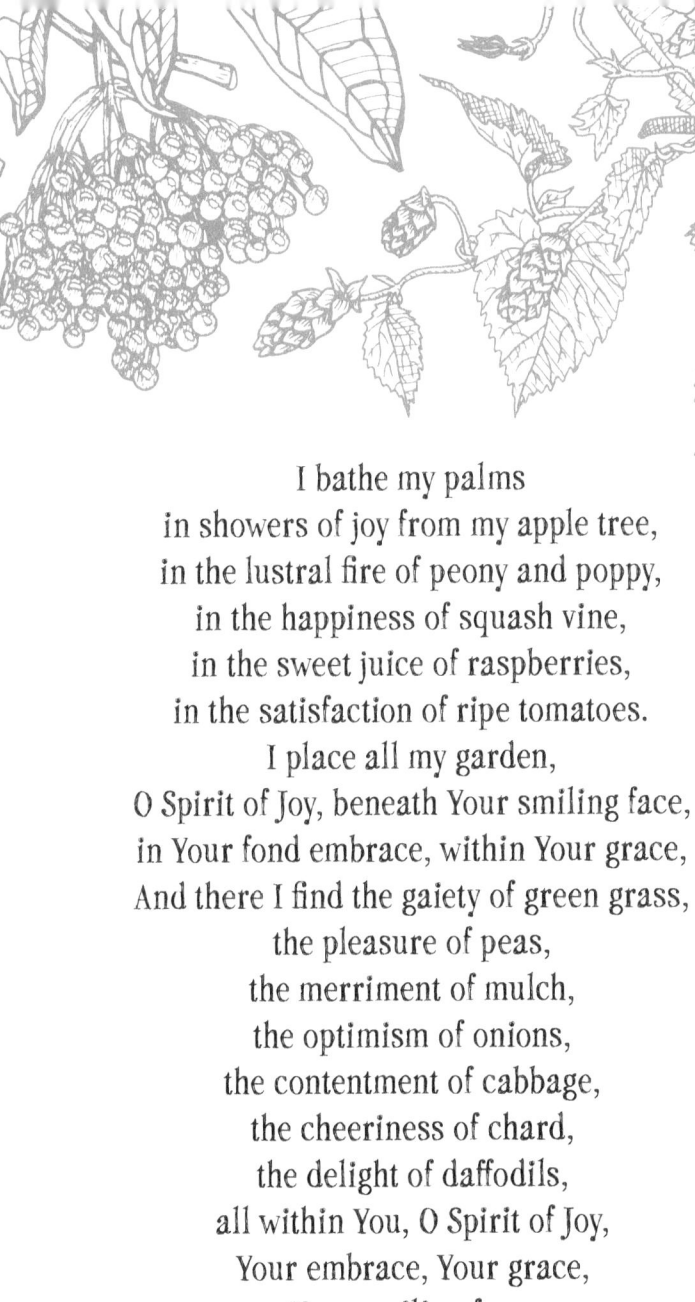

I bathe my palms
in showers of joy from my apple tree,
in the lustral fire of peony and poppy,
in the happiness of squash vine,
in the sweet juice of raspberries,
in the satisfaction of ripe tomatoes.
I place all my garden,
O Spirit of Joy, beneath Your smiling face,
in Your fond embrace, within Your grace,
And there I find the gaiety of green grass,
the pleasure of peas,
the merriment of mulch,
the optimism of onions,
the contentment of cabbage,
the cheeriness of chard,
the delight of daffodils,
all within You, O Spirit of Joy,
Your embrace, Your grace,
Your smiling face.

The air and genius of gardens . . .
do influence the soul and spirits of man,
and prepare them for
converse with good angels.

—JOHN EVELYN

Our notion of what makes a paradise
always returns to the image
of a beautiful and fruitful garden.

—JEFF COX

How could such sweet and wholesome hours
Be reckon'd, but with herbs and flowers!

—ANDREW MARVEL

To see a world in a grain of sand
and heaven in a flower;
hold infinity in the palm of your hand
and eternity in an hour.

—WILLIAM BLAKE

I used to visit and revisit it a dozen times a day, and stand in deep contemplation over my vegetable progeny with a love that nobody could share or conceive of who had never taken part in the process of creation. It was one of the most bewitching sights in the world to observe a hill of beans thrusting aside the soil, or a row of early peas just peeping forth sufficiently to trace a line of delicate green.

—NATHANIEL HAWTHORNE

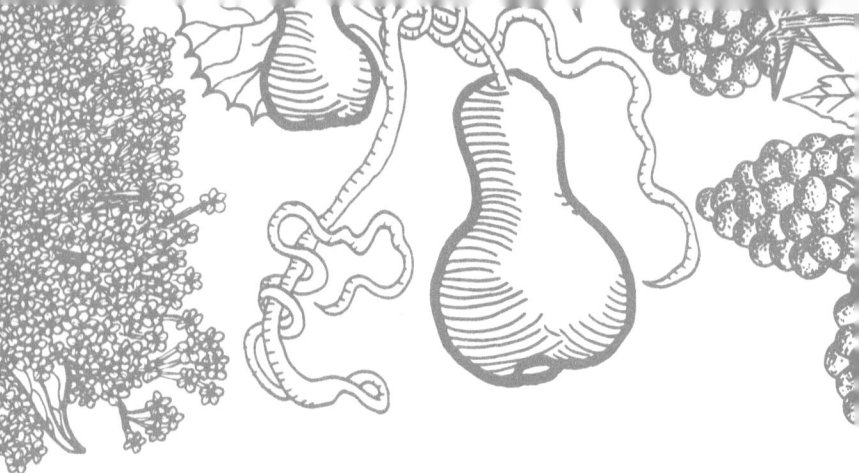

One by one our senses are captivated
and charmed by the garden
and then all together:
we are swimming in birdsong
and perfume, fresh flavor
and cool touches,
all decorated with gorgeous colors.

—JEFF COX

What I enjoy is not the fruit alone,
but I also enjoy the soil itself.

—CICERO

The flowers take the tears of weeping night,
And give them to the sun for the day's delight.

—JOSEPH S. COTTER SR.

Earth-voices are glad voices,
and earth-songs come up from the ground
through the plants.

—OPAL WHITELEY

The first gathering of salads,
radishes and herbs made me feel
like a mother about her baby—
how could anything so beautiful be mine?

—ALICE B. TOKLAS

Who loves a garden still Eden keeps.

—A. BRONSON ALCOTT

Whoever understands and loves a garden
may have contentment.

—CHINESE PROVERB

Forsythia is pure joy.
There is not an ounce,
not a glimmer of sadness . . . in forsythia.

—ANNE MORROW LINDBERGH

What is all this juice and all this joy?
A strain of earth's sweet being
in the beginning
In Eden garden.

—GERARD MANLEY HOPKINS

Spirit of Joy,
a shade art Thou in the heat,
a shelter art Thou in the cold,
eyes art Thou to the blind,
a staff art Thou to the pilgrim,
an island art Thou at sea,
a fortress art Thou on land,
a well art Thou in the desert,
health art Thou to the ailing,
O great Spirit of Joy.

> 'Tis my faith that every flower
> Enjoys the air it breathes!
>
> —WILLIAM WORDSWORTH

There is only a single, urgent task: to attach oneself someplace to nature, to that which is strong, striving and bright with unreserved readiness, and then to move forward in one's efforts.... Each time we thus reach out with joy, each time we cast our view toward distances that have not yet been touched, we transform not only the present moment and the one following but we also alter the past within us, weave it into the pattern of our existence....

—RAINER MARIA RILKE

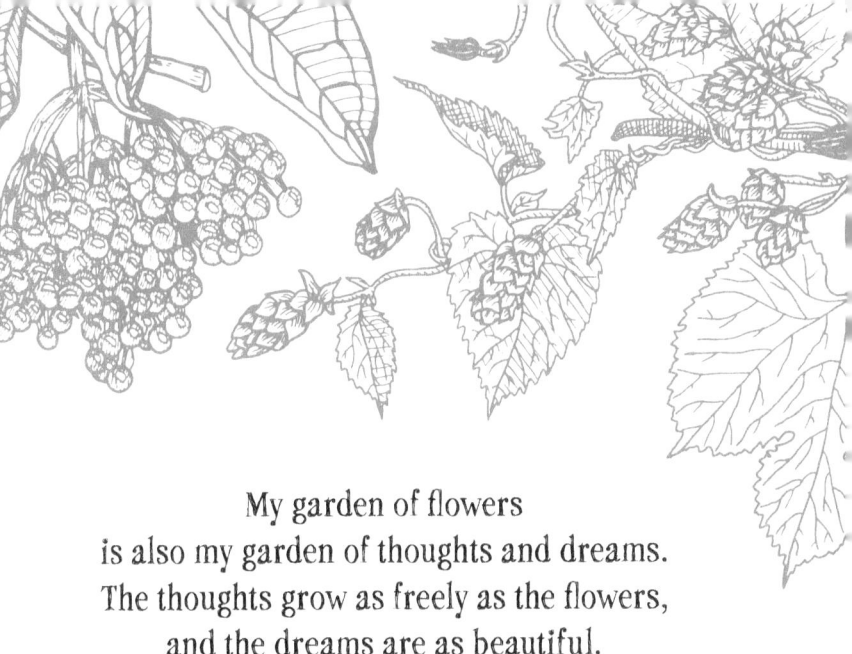

My garden of flowers
is also my garden of thoughts and dreams.
The thoughts grow as freely as the flowers,
and the dreams are as beautiful.

—ABRAM L. URBAN

I will be the gladdest thing
Under the sun!
I will touch a hundred flowers
And not pick one.

—EDNA ST. VINCENT MILLAY

3

THE CREATIVITY OF THE GARDEN

I cultivate my garden,
and my garden cultivates me.

—ROBERT BRAULT

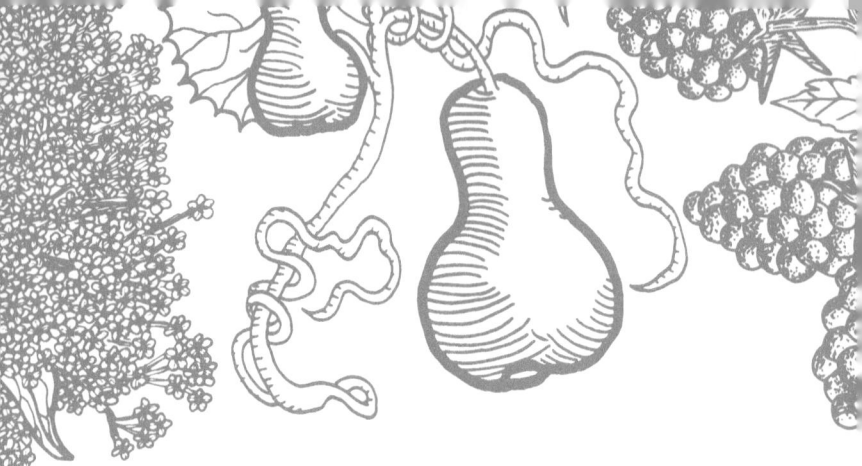

I have never had so many good ideas
day after day
as when I worked in the garden.

—JOHN ERSKINE

All work is as seed sown;
it grows and spreads,
and sows itself anew.

—THOMAS CARLYLE

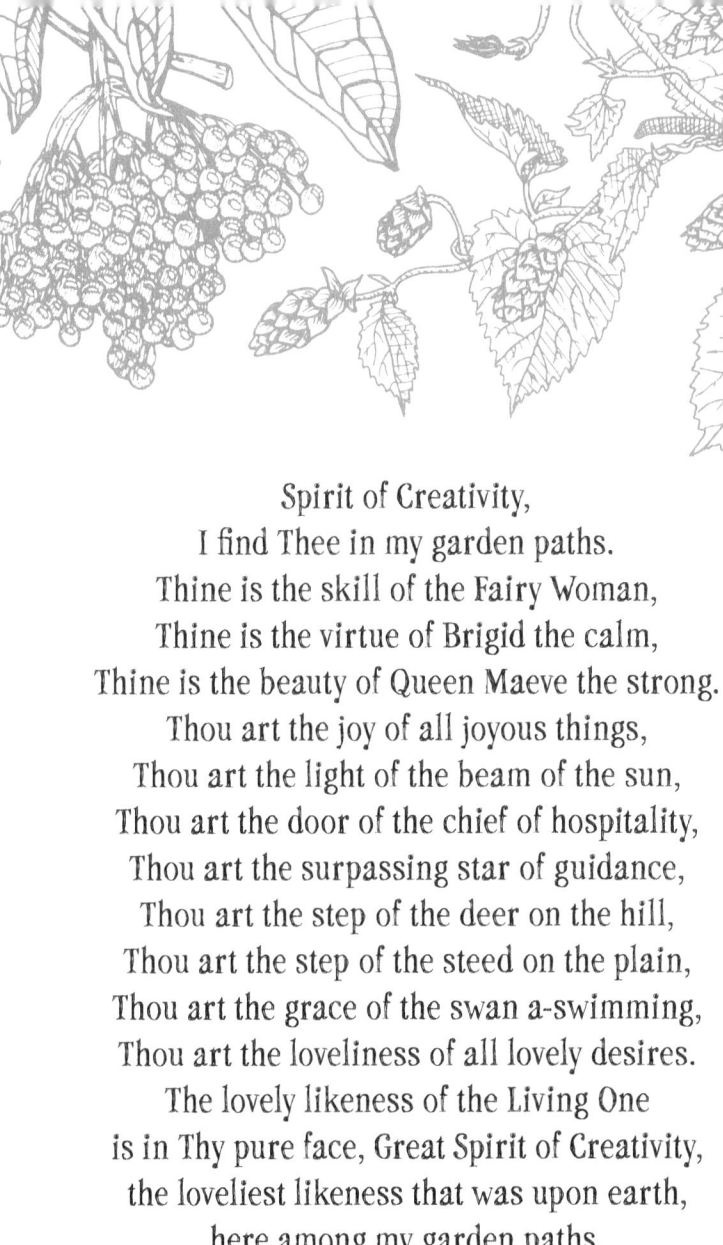

Spirit of Creativity,
I find Thee in my garden paths.
Thine is the skill of the Fairy Woman,
Thine is the virtue of Brigid the calm,
Thine is the beauty of Queen Maeve the strong.
Thou art the joy of all joyous things,
Thou art the light of the beam of the sun,
Thou art the door of the chief of hospitality,
Thou art the surpassing star of guidance,
Thou art the step of the deer on the hill,
Thou art the step of the steed on the plain,
Thou art the grace of the swan a-swimming,
Thou art the loveliness of all lovely desires.
The lovely likeness of the Living One
is in Thy pure face, Great Spirit of Creativity,
the loveliest likeness that was upon earth,
here among my garden paths.

It is the marriage of the soul with Nature
that makes the intellect fruitful
and gives birth to imagination.

—HENRY DAVID THOREAU

I perhaps owe having become
a painter to flowers.

—CLAUDE MONET

In the art of gardening, artists lay out the work and devise a garment for a piece of ground, have the delight of seeing their work live and grow hour by hour; and, while it is growing, they are able to polish, to cut and carve, to fill up here and there, to hope, and to love.

— PRINCE ALBERT

We have neglected the truth
that a good farmer is a craftsman
of the highest order, a kind of artist.

— WENDELL BERRY

Creativity is a green and living thing.
Its expression goes out into the world,
but I find that it grows best secretly,
privately, within my garden.

—**URSULA ELLIOTT**

Alone in my garden,
enclosed within its walls,
my creativity has room to wander.
She spreads her wings, unafraid to fly,
and afterward, I return to my desk to write,
my fingers faster, my mind more focused,
my spirit quieter, my imagination more fertile.

—**MARJORIE BENNET**

Spirit of Creativity,
the best hour of the day be Thine,
the best day of the week be Thine,
the best week of the year be Thine,
the best year in Thy great domain be Thine.
Amid both daffodil and aster,
between tender lettuce leaves
and swelling pumpkins,
teach me, Spirit of Creativity,
to follow in Thy paths.

4

LESSONS OF THE GARDEN

Listen to Nature's teachings.

—WILLIAM CULLEN BRYANT

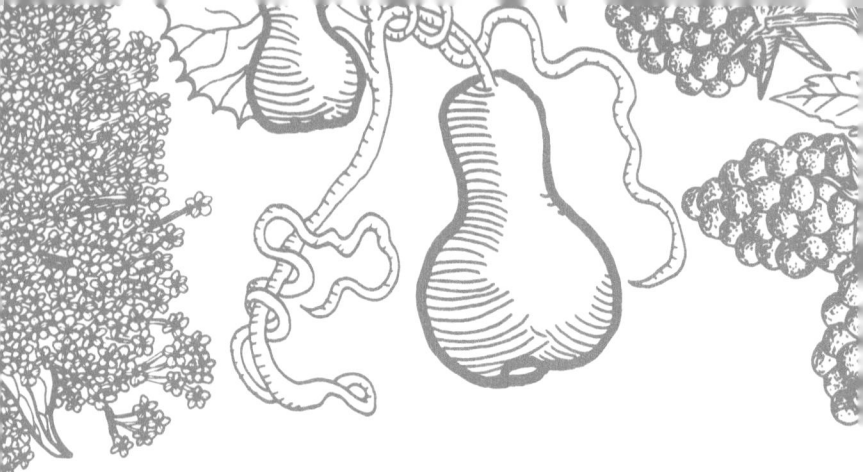

A garden is a grand teacher.
It teaches patience
and careful watchfulness;
it teaches industry and thrift;
above all it teaches entire trust.

—GERTRUDE JEKYLL

In a thousand unseen ways
we have drawn shape
and strength from the land.

—LYNDON B. JOHNSON

Who bends a knee when violets grow,
a hundred secret things shall know.

—RACHEL FIELD

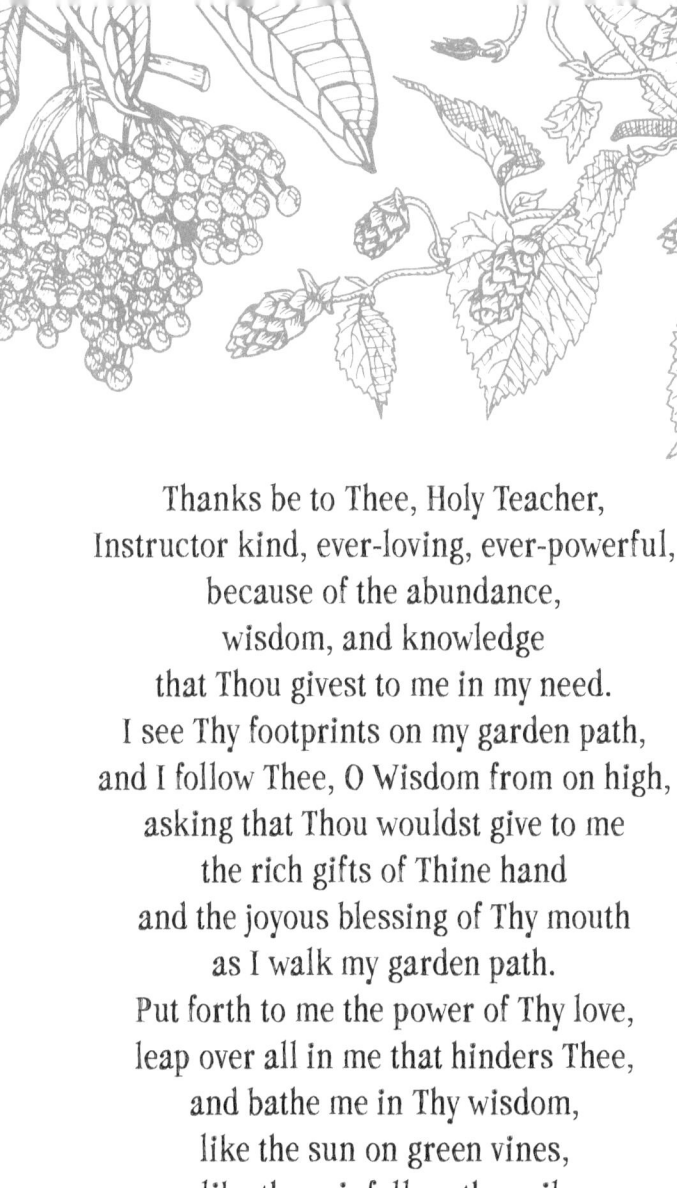

Thanks be to Thee, Holy Teacher,
Instructor kind, ever-loving, ever-powerful,
because of the abundance,
wisdom, and knowledge
that Thou givest to me in my need.
I see Thy footprints on my garden path,
and I follow Thee, O Wisdom from on high,
asking that Thou wouldst give to me
the rich gifts of Thine hand
and the joyous blessing of Thy mouth
as I walk my garden path.
Put forth to me the power of Thy love,
leap over all in me that hinders Thee,
and bathe me in Thy wisdom,
like the sun on green vines,
like the rainfall on the soil.

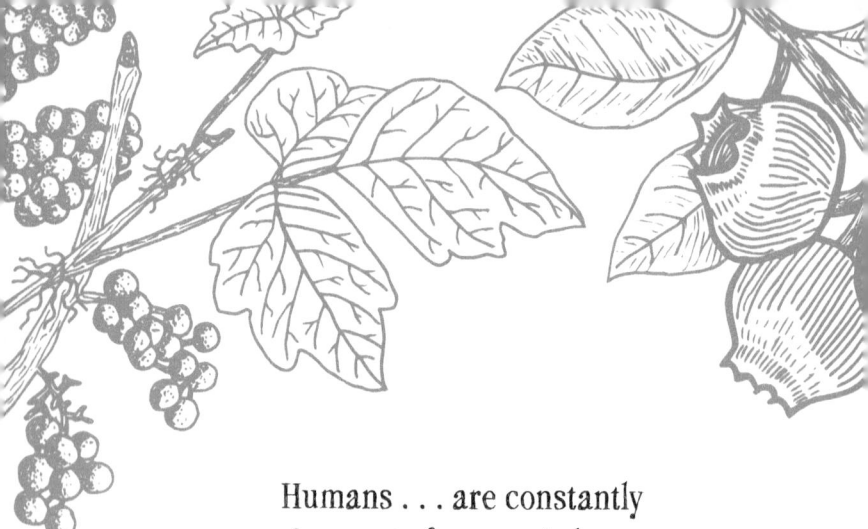

Humans . . . are constantly
in quest of more wisdom;
but the ultimate wisdom,
which deals with beginnings,
remains locked in a seed.

—HAL BORLAND

All flowers talk to me
and so do hundreds
of little living things in the woods.
I learn what I know by watching
and loving everything.

—GEORGE WASHINGTON CARVER

Nature's lessons
will remain opaque
as long as we are full
of our own ideas
and preconceptions.

—JEFF COX

A modest garden contains,
for those who know how to look and wait,
more instruction than a library.

—HENRI FRÉDÉRIC AMIEL

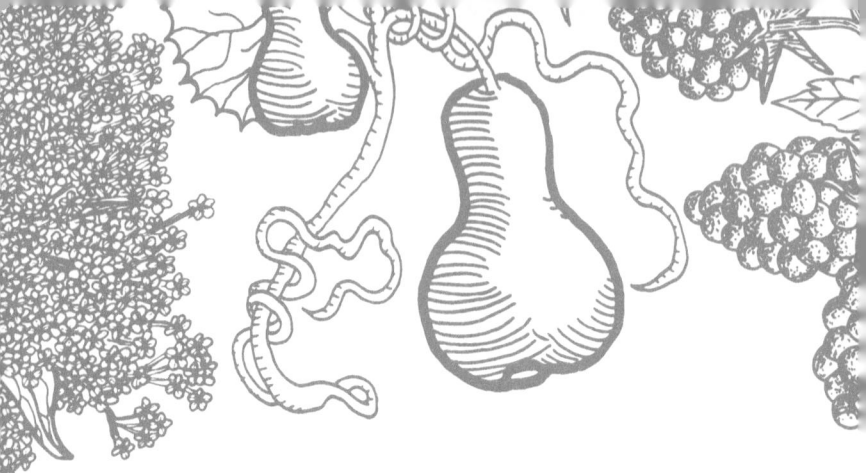

Basic to an integrated life is a dominant idea.
To plow a straight row, we must keep
our eyes on the goal rather than the plow.

—J. M. PRICE

The more one gardens,
the more one learns;
and the more one learns,
the more one realizes
how little one knows.
I suppose the whole of life is like that.

—V. SACKVILLE-WEST

A morning-glory at my window
satisfies me more than
the metaphysics of books.

—WALT WHITMAN

Eventually, a gardener
becomes a philosopher.

—BARBARA DODGE BORLAND

Give me a spark of Nature's fire.
That's all the learning I desire.

—ROBERT BURNS

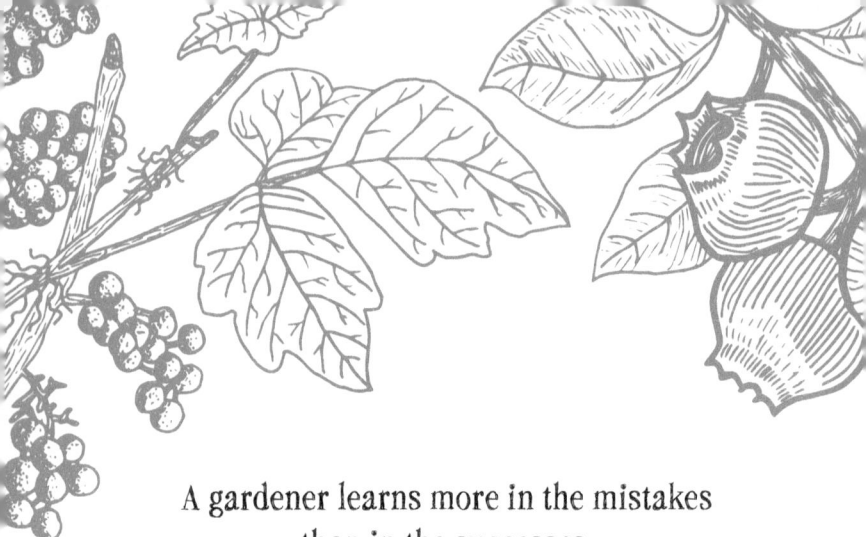

A gardener learns more in the mistakes
than in the successes.

— **BARBARA DODGE BORLAND**

In the steep common path of our calling,
be it easy or uneasy to our flesh,
be it bright or dark for us to follow,
Thine own perfect guidance be upon us.
Teach us the wisdom that grows
with leaf and flower.
May I learn from the flexibility
of stem and branch,
the courage of blossoms in the rain.
Give us open hearts and open minds
to learn from every leaf and flower,
as we follow the steep path of our calling.

Consider the lilies of the field,
how they grow; they toil not,
neither do they spin.
And yet I say unto you,
that even Solomon in all his glory
was not arrayed like one of these.

—JESUS

5

THE HUMILITY, PATIENCE, & FAITH OF GARDENING

There is nothing more humble, patient, or full of faith than a seed lying in the soil, waiting for the spring.

—URSULA ELLIOTT

Despite the gardener's best intentions,
Nature will improvise.

— MICHAEL P. GARAFALO

Many things grow in the garden
that were never sown there.

— THOMAS FULLER

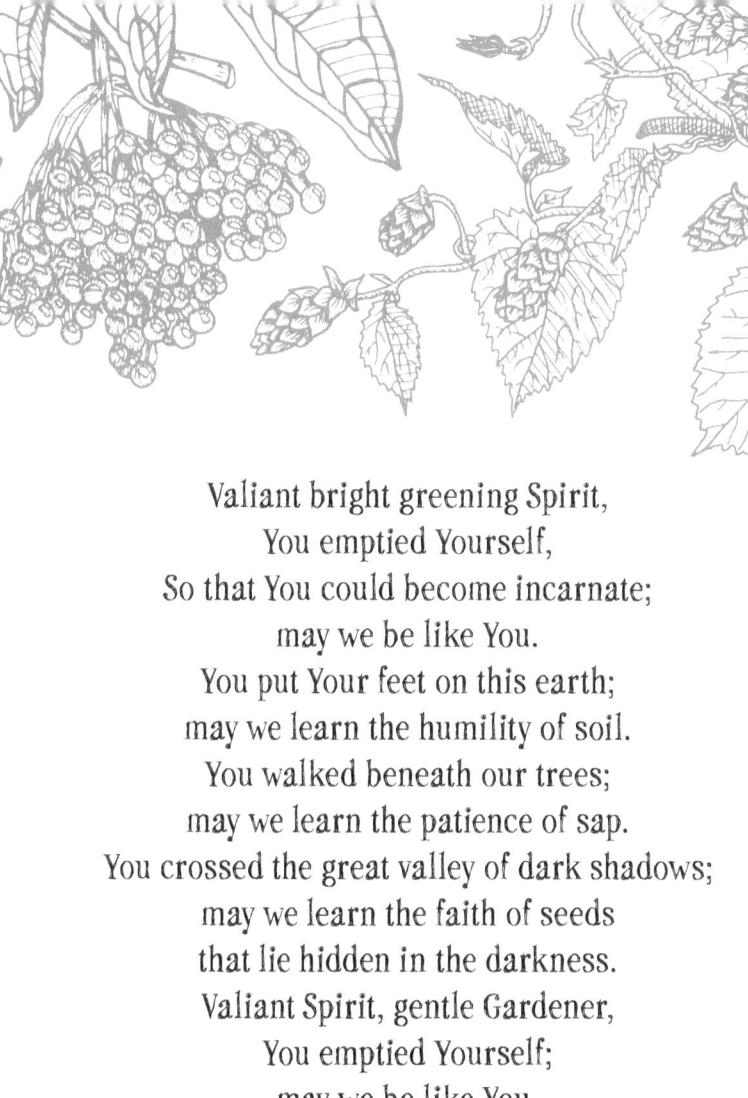

Valiant bright greening Spirit,
You emptied Yourself,
So that You could become incarnate;
may we be like You.
You put Your feet on this earth;
may we learn the humility of soil.
You walked beneath our trees;
may we learn the patience of sap.
You crossed the great valley of dark shadows;
may we learn the faith of seeds
that lie hidden in the darkness.
Valiant Spirit, gentle Gardener,
You emptied Yourself;
may we be like You.

A garden is moved by influences
you cannot see, fully comprehend
or control. You are only part
of the whole blooming thing.

— **JAMIE JOBB**

There is no gardening without humility.
Nature is constantly sending
even its oldest scholars
to the bottom of the class
for some egregious blunder.

— **ALFRED AUSTIN**

Adam was a gardener,
and God who made him sees
that half a proper gardener's work
is done upon his knees.

—RUDYARD KIPLING

Sweet flowers are slow.

—WILLIAM SHAKESPEARE

Adapt the pace of nature:
her secret is patience.

—RALPH WALDO EMERSON

The greatest prayer is patience.

— THE BUDDHA

Now to the Creator who shapes each creature,
now to the One who ever lives,
now to the Holy Breath, Comforter of all,
I ask You grant me patience
to run my race, from the beginning to the end.
May I learn from my garden's plants
the quietness of patience,
the beauty of endurance,
the fertility of waiting.
May I grow in Your Garden,
in Your time, at Your pace.

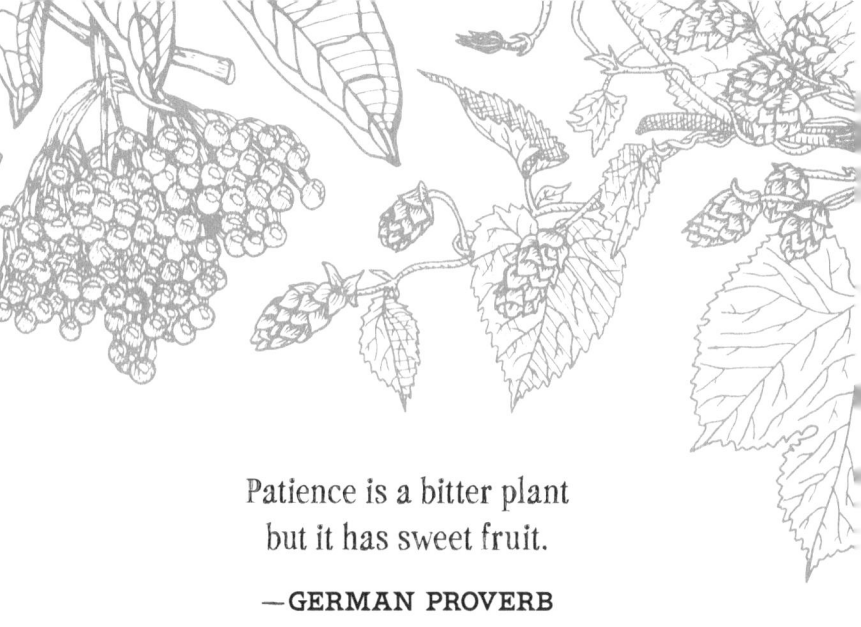

Patience is a bitter plant
but it has sweet fruit.

—GERMAN PROVERB

Bring forth fruit with patience.

—JESUS

The only thing different
about having a green thumb
is that you don't get discouraged by failure.
When something doesn't work,
you try again.

—BETH WEIDNER

Who has learned to garden
who did not at the same time
learn to be patient?

—H. L. V. FLETCHER

The garden that is finished
is dead.

—H. E. BATES

Gardening helps us realize somatically, viscerally, the laws of growth and gradual unfolding. We can't pull the plants up to make them grow, but we can help facilitate and midwife their blooming, each in his own way, time, and proper season. I have learned a little about patience and humility from my gardens. It's so obviously not something I'm doing that creates this miracle!

—LAMA SURYA DAS

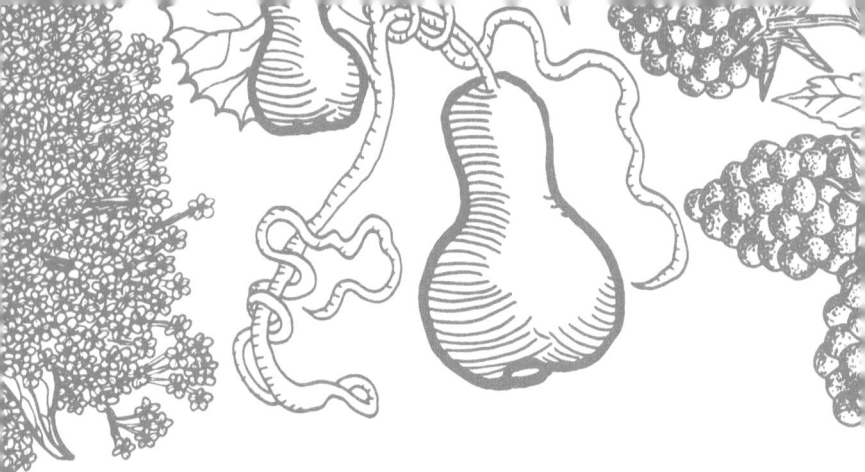

The garden is inimical to all evil passion:
it stands for efficiency,
for patience in labour,
for strength in adversary,
for the power to forgive.

—GEORGE SITWELL

True gardeners are lover of their flowers, not the critics of them. I think the true gardener is the reverent servant of Nature, not her truculent, wife-beating master. I think true gardeners, the older they grow, should more and more develop a humble, grateful and uncertain spirit.

— REGINALD FARRER

Putting in an asparagus bed
is like planting a tree.
The hard work comes at the beginning,
and you need faith in the future
to accomplish it.

—ELEANOR PERENYI

O Creator Spirit,
in my deeds,
in my words,
in my wishes,
in my reason,
and in the fulfilling of my desires;
in my sleep,
in my dreams,
in my repose,
in my thoughts,
in my heart and soul always,
may the seed of faith grow,
and the promised Branch of Glory dwell.
May the seed of faith sprout and leaf,
and the fragrant Branch of Glory dwell.

6

HEALING IN THE GARDEN

All my hurts
my garden spade can heal.

—RALPH WALDO EMERSON

The greatest gift of the garden
is the restoration of the five senses.

— HANNA RION

Gardening is cheaper than therapy
and you get tomatoes.

— AUTHOR UNKNOWN

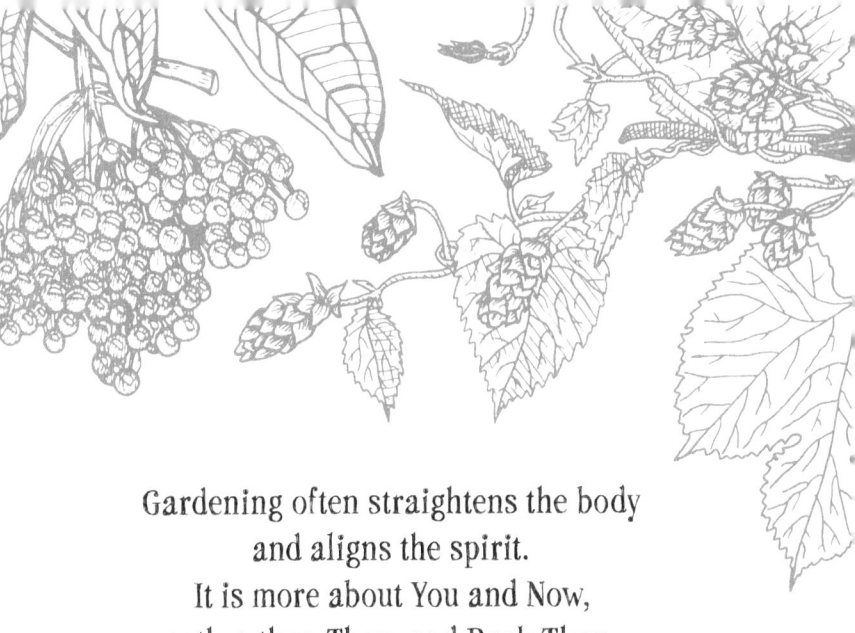

Gardening often straightens the body
and aligns the spirit.
It is more about You and Now,
rather than Them and Back Then.

—MICHAEL P. GAROFALO

What is it about gardening
that works out something bad?

—ANNE CHOTZINOFF GROSSMAN

An hour's digging is a good way
of getting one's mind back
in the right perspective.

— RICHARD BRIERS

In smoothing the rough hillocks,
I smooth my temper.

— RALPH WALDO EMERSON

The highest reward for our toil
is not what we get for it
but what we become by it.

— JOHN RUSKIN

Thou, Spirit of the moon,
Thou, Spirit of the sun,
Thou, Spirit of the Earth,
Thou, Spirit of the stars,
Thou, Spirit of the grass,
Thou, Spirit of tree and leaf,
of flower and fruit,
grant me, I pray, Thy healing.
Thou, Spirit of my garden,
Oh! lovely Thy countenance,
Thou beauteous Beam,
heal me I pray.

Once we become interested
in the progress of the plants in our care,
their development becomes a part
of the rhythm of our own lives
and we are refreshed by it.

—**THALASSA CRUSO**

There is something about sun and soil
that heals broken bodies
and jangled nerves.

—**NATURE MAGAZINE**

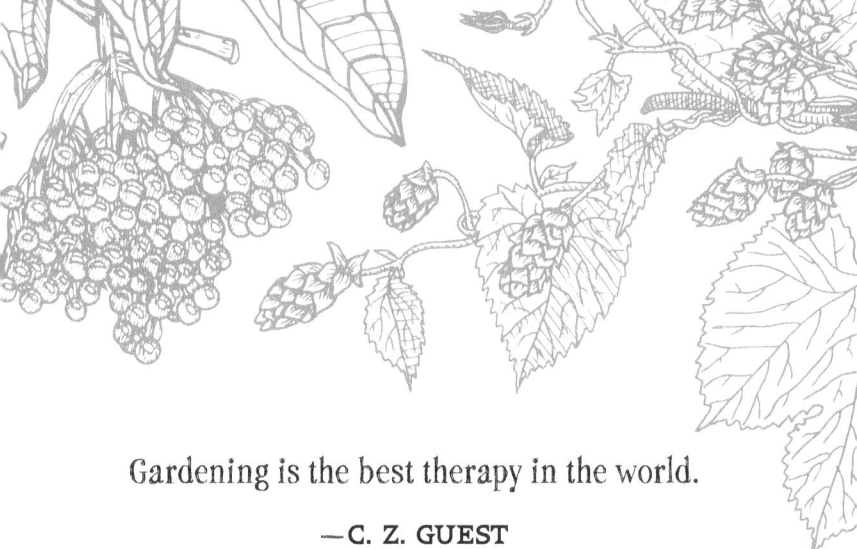

Gardening is the best therapy in the world.

—C. Z. GUEST

The soil is the great connector of lives, the source and destination of all. It is the healer and restorer and resurrector, by which disease passes into health, age into youth, death into life. Without proper care for it we can have no community, because without proper care for it we can have no life.

—WENDELL BERRY

HEALING IN THE GARDEN

Bless me, O Spirit of Healing,
myself and everything anear me.
Bless me in all my actions,
and heal me in each thought.
Make me safe forever
from every evil wish and sorrow,
from every troll among the hills,
from every ghoul within the glens,
from every hint of hatred within my heart.
O green Spirit, heal me day by day!
O heal me day by day!

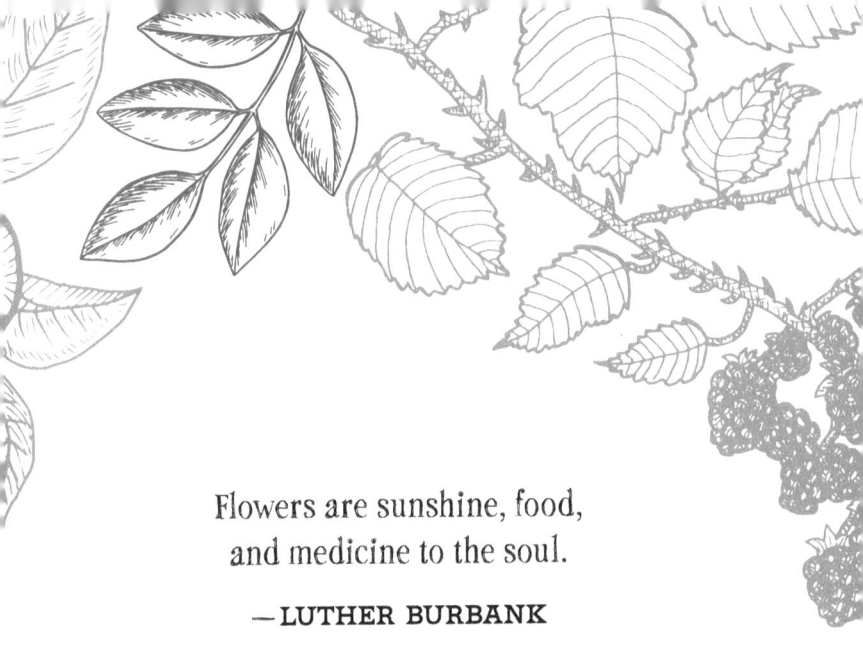

Flowers are sunshine, food,
and medicine to the soul.

—LUTHER BURBANK

Bread feeds the body,
but flowers feed the soul.

—THE QUR'AN

7

THE MIRACLE OF GARDENING

If we could see the miracle
of a single flower clearly
our whole life would change.

—THE BUDDHA

Of all the wonderful things
in the wonderful universe of God,
nothing seems to me more surprising
than the planting of a seed
in the blank earth
and the result thereof.

—JULIE MOIR MESSERVY

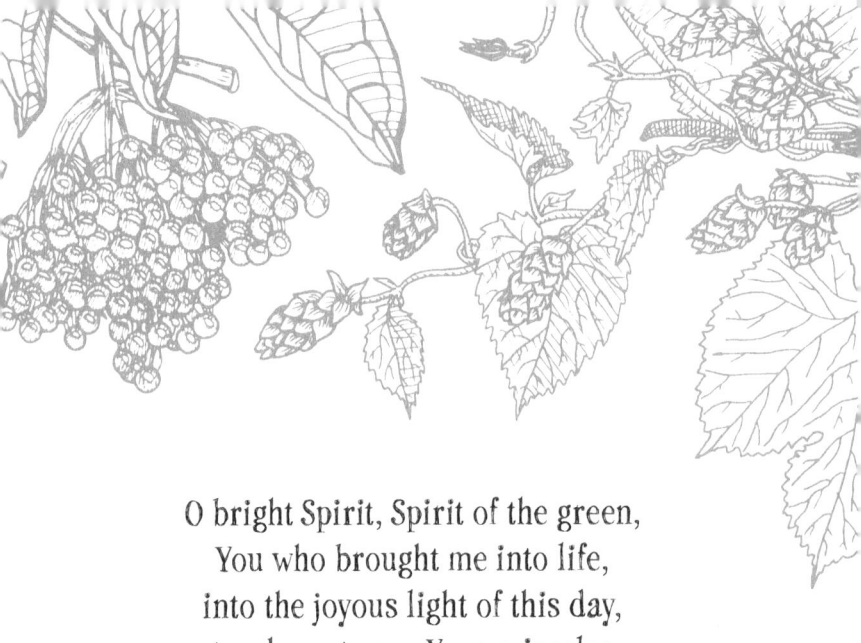

O bright Spirit, Spirit of the green,
You who brought me into life,
into the joyous light of this day,
teach me to see Your miracles
springing like grass beneath my feet,
opening like dandelions to the sun.
Be to me the guiding light of eternity.
Oh! from the new light of this day
into the guiding light of eternity.

Anything will give up its secrets if you love
it enough. Not only have I found that when
I talk to the little flower or to the little peanut
they will give up their secrets, but I have
found that when I silently commune with
people they give up their secrets also—
if you love them enough.

   —**GEORGE WASHINGTON CARVER**

How miraculous that growing
on my own little plot of land
are plants that can turn the dead soil
into a hundred flavours
as different as horseradish and thyme,
smells ranging from stinkhorn to lavender.

   —**JOHN SEYMOUR**

Put in the plow
and plant the great hereafter
in the now.

— ROBERT FROST

The word "miracle" aptly describes a seed.

— JACK KRAMER

A grass-blade's no easier
to make than an oak.

— JAMES RUSSELL LOWELL

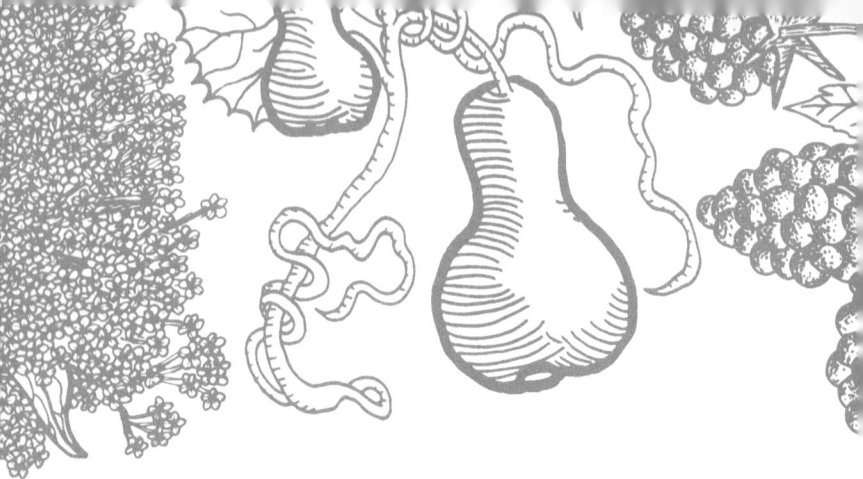

Beauty can inspire miracles.

—BENJAMIN DISRAELI

At the heart of gardening
there is a belief in the miraculous.

—MIRABEL OSLER

Every leaf a miracle.

—WALT WHITMAN

Every gardener knows
under the cloak of winter lies a miracle—
a seed waiting to sprout,
a bulb opening to light,
a bud straining to unfurl.
And the anticipation nurtures our dream.

—BARBARA WINKLER

Into every empty corner,
into all forgotten things and nooks,
Nature struggles to pour life,
pouring life into the dead,
life into life itself.

—HENRY BESTON

I have great faith in a seed.
Convince me that you have a seed there,
and I am prepared to expect wonders.

— **HENRY DAVID THOREAU**

What Nature delivers to us is never stale,
because what Nature creates
has eternity in it.

— **ISAAC BASHEVIS SINGER**

A garden is a place of ordinary,
daily miracles
that point our attention
from Earth to Heaven.

— **URSULA ELLIOTT**

The only words that ever satisfied me
as describing Nature are the terms
used in fairy books, "charm,"
"spell," "enchantment."

—G. K. CHESTERTON

Every morning, I half expect
to see fairies peeping out
between my garden rows.

—JIM G. BROWN

I had never "taken a cutting" before. . . . Do you realize that the whole thing is miraculous? It is exactly as though you were to cut off your wife's leg, stick it in the lawn, and be greeted on the following day by an entirely new woman, sprung from the leg, advancing across the lawn to meet you.

—BEVERLEY NICHOLS

I am bending my knee
in the miracle of the Living One
who created me,
in the miracle of the green Spirit
who lives in me,
in the miracle of One who is Love.
Pour down upon us the miracles
of greenness and growth,
the rich blessing of life,
the fertile blessing of green life,
O Living One, O green Spirit, O Love.

When I open up my seed packets,
who would think what wonders
would grow from these small objects—
cabbages, peppers, marigolds,
tomatoes, and nasturtium.
Amazing!

—**URSULA ELLIOTT**

It were as easy for You, Living Spirit
to renew the withered tree
as to renew my own heart.
There is no plant in the ground
but is full of Your miracles;
there is no form in the strand
but is full of Your blessing.
There is no life in the sea,
there is no creature in the river,
there is naught in the firmament,
but proclaims Your goodness.
There is no bird on the wing,
there is no star in the sky,
there is nothing beneath the sun,
but proclaims the miracle of Life.

8

HUMANS & NATURE IN THE GARDEN

The garden is a love song,
a duet between a
human being and Nature.

—JEFF COX

We master nature not by force
but by understanding.

—JACOB BRONOWSKI

The soil is a wonderful thing.
Treat it like a good old friend.

—FRED STREETER

Think about the garden
as a small community
of plants and animals
coexisting with one another
and with human beings.

—RUTH SHAW ERNST

Grant to us, O Spirit of the Earth,
sorrow for all the ways
we have caused you harm.
Teach us to guard you, to heal you.
May we be the hands of the Living One,
working with you to bring back
beauty to our world.
Teach us to guard you, to heal you.

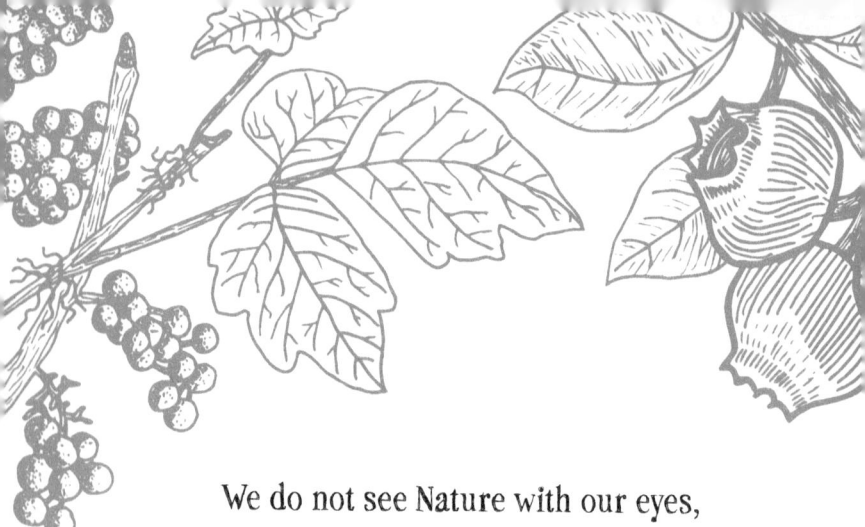

We do not see Nature with our eyes,
but with our understanding
and with our hearts.

—WILLIAM HAZLITT

Touch the earth, love the earth,
honour the earth.

—HENRY BESTON

Nature will bear the closest inspection.
She invites us to lay our eye level
with her smallest leaf,
and take an insect's view.

—HENRY DAVID THOREAU

Confronted with the vision
of a beautiful garden, we see
something beautiful about ourselves,
as part of Nature.

—JEFF COX

Flowers supply our souls
with the beauty that is necessary
to keep our thoughts
in tune with Nature.

—JIM G. BROWN

Awareness of the continuous process
of birth, growth, bloom, decay,
and renewal gives rise to a feeling of kinship
with all living things.

—RUTH SHAW ERNST

Nobody sees a flower—really—
it's so small. It takes time—
we haven't time—
and to see takes time,
like to have a friend takes time.

—GEORGIA O'KEEFFE

Spirit, bless the world and all that is therein.
Spirit, bless the good soil and all that grows in it.
Spirit, bless the eye that sees in my head,
and bless, O God, the work of my hand.
May I do my small part
to bring healing to Thy Earth.
Spirit, protect the Earth and all that grows on her.
Spirit, consecrate the children
of humanity to do Thy will.
Spirit, encompass all creatures and their young.
Be Thou around them and tending them,
and may I work with Thee
to bring healing to Thy Earth,
both here in my small garden plot
and throughout the green globe.
Spirit, bless the world and all that is therein.
May I do my small part
to bring healing to Thy Earth.

Most people don't see the sun,
soil, bugs, seeds, plants, moon,
water, clouds, and wind
the way gardeners do.

—JAMIE JOBB

The spontaneous energies
of the earth are a gift of nature,
but they require human labors
to direct their operation.

—THOMAS JEFFERSON

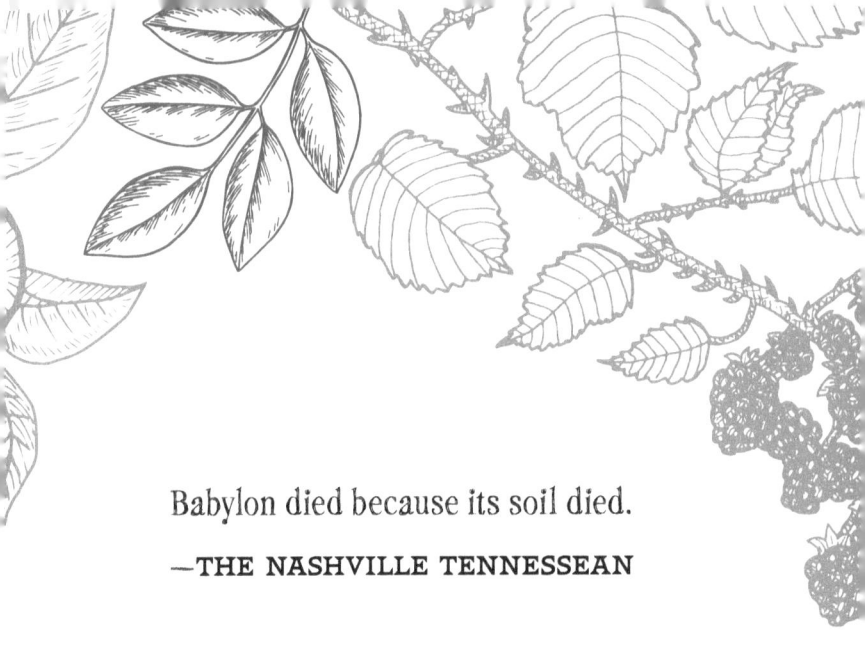

Babylon died because its soil died.

—THE NASHVILLE TENNESSEAN

The farmer who takes everything
from the land without restitution
will become the servant of wiser folk.

—C. E. THORNE

As You are the green Spirit over all the Earth,
tend now my plot of land.
Guard it beneath Your own glorious mantle.
Teach me to bring forth beauty
on this small plot of land,
and may I work as hard for all the Earth,
to tend and guard and bring forth beauty.
Shield of Protection, guard our land,
from the smoke of pollution
and the dirt of garbage.
Protect and heal her atmosphere.
May Archangel Michael come to her defense.
Shield of Protection, tend now my plot of land.
Shield of Protection, guard all the Earth.

We are here to cultivate the garden
and take care of it.

—GENESIS 2:15

The Earth is our mother,
She cares for us.
The Earth is our mother,
we care for Her.

—FIRST NATIONS SAYING

9

TIME & THE GARDEN

A garden is a link
to the passing of seasons.

—SHERYL LONDON

Here is the great mystery
of life and growth:
Everything is changing, growing,
aiming at something, but silently,
unboastfully, taking its time.

—RUTH STOUT

On the Rock of rocks,
time stands still.
The circle cycles 'round us,
the ever-changing seasons,
the leaves that turn from green
to scarlet to brown,
just as one day our bodies too
shall drop away, spent, no longer needed.
Only You remain the same,
the still point at the center.
In You is peace, Creator of joy.
In You is peace, Child of new birth.
In You is peace, Spirit of ever-green,
to ourselves and to our children,
ourselves and our children
and our children's children.

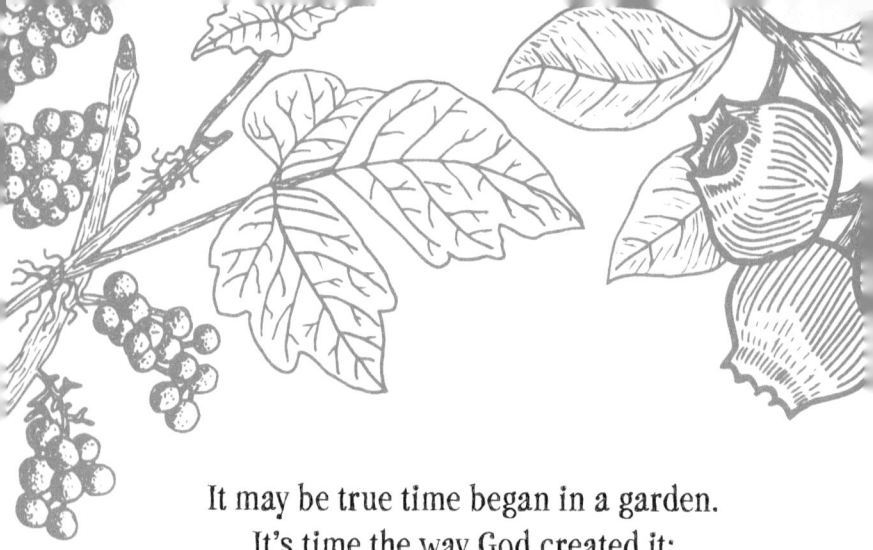

It may be true time began in a garden.
It's time the way God created it:
as servant, not master.

—EMILIE BARNES

Things seem to move
very slowly in a garden.
But nothing ever remains the same.

—JAMIE JOBB

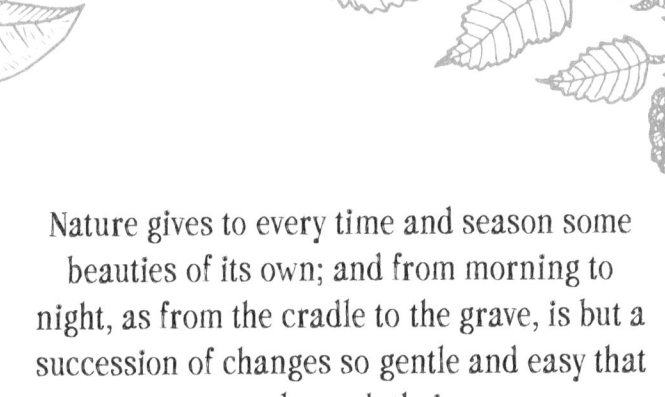

Nature gives to every time and season some beauties of its own; and from morning to night, as from the cradle to the grave, is but a succession of changes so gentle and easy that we can scarcely mark their progress.

—**CHARLES DICKENS**

Come to the garden,
The soul's sweet bouquet.
The flowers of tomorrow
Are in the seeds of today.

—**JOANNA O'KEEFE**

Though nothing can bring back the hour
Of splendor in the grass, of glory in the flower,
We will grieve not, rather find
Strength in what remains behind.

—**WILLIAM WORDSWORTH**

No winter lasts forever,
no spring skips its turn.
April is a promise
that May is bound to keep.

—HAL BORLAND

Behold the One who lights the stars
who rides on the crests of the clouds,
who sings with the birds in the sky,
a timeless song of praise.
O refuge from time, never-changing,
always young, ever-green,
bringing new birth from death,
O exceeding white purity of beauty,
joy were it to me to be in the fields
to see the loveliness of my garden,
to know that death is never final.

Oh this is the joy of the rose—
that it blooms and goes.

—WILLA CATHER

God gave us memories
that we might have roses in December.

—J. M. BARRIE

10

GOD IN THE GARDEN

In the cool of the day,
God was walking in the garden.

—GENESIS 3:8

The best place to seek God is in a garden.
You can dig for him there.

—GEORGE BERNARD SHAW

Beauty is God's handwriting.
Welcome it in every fair face,
every fair sky, every fair flower.

—CHARLES KINGSLEY

What greater delight is there than to behold the earth appareled with plants, as with a robe of embroidered work. . . ? But these delights are in the outward senses; the principal delight is in the mind, singularly enriched with the knowledge of these visible things, setting forth to us the invisible wisdom and admirable workmanship of Almighty God.

—JOHN GERARD

Thou angel of my garden,
from the dear Creator of mercifulness,
the shepherd kind of each plant and flower,
drive from me every temptation and danger,
surround me with thy bright spirit,
and in the narrows, crooks, and straits,
keep thou my little boat, keep it always.
Be thou a bright flame before me,
be thou a guiding star above me,
be thou a smooth path below me,
and be a kindly shepherd behind me,
today, tonight, and forever.
I am tired and my heart is heavy;
lead thou me from my garden paths
to the land of angels;
I am longing to go home,
to find here in my garden green
the peace of heaven
and the Presence of the Life-Giver.

A garden is a lovesome thing. . .
The veriest school
Of peace; and yet the fool
Contends that God is not—
Not God! in gardens! When the eve is cool?
Nay, but I have a sign;
'Tis very sure God walks in mine.

—T. E. BROWN

Never lose an opportunity
of seeing anything that is beautiful,
for beauty is God's handwriting—
a wayside sacrament.

—RALPH WALDO EMERSON

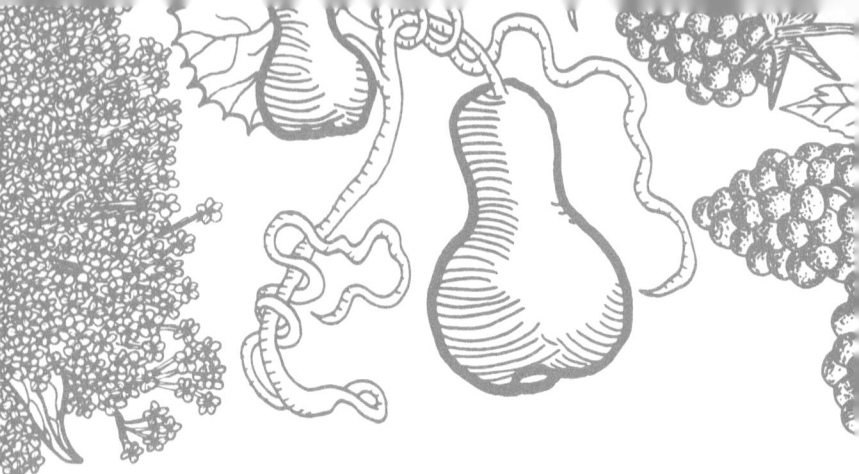

Gardening is an instrument of grace.

—**MAY SARTON**

Heaven is under our feet
as well as over our heads.

—**HENRY DAVID THOREAU**

Nature is the living,
visible garment of God.

—**JOHANN WOLFGANG VON GOETHE**

See Nature, and through her, God.

—HENRY DAVID THOREAU

Behold! the Holy Grail is found,
Found in each poppy's cup of gold;
And God walks with us as of old.

—JOAQUIN MILLER

God in the whizzing of a pleasant wind
Shall march upon the tops of mulberry trees.

—GEORGE PEELE

In this light, my spirit saw through all things
and into all creatures,
and I recognized God in grass and plants.

—JACOB BOEHME

Flowers are peculiarly the poetry of Christ.

—CHRISTOPHER SMART

In quiet moments in my garden,
may I sense Thy Presence
and then go forth into my life,
to speak each day according to Thy justice;
may I speak each day
according to Thy wisdom,
and then return to times of solitude here
with Thee in my garden green.

Each day and night may I
be at peace with Thee.
Each day may I count the causes of Thy mercy,
each day may I compose for Thee a song.
May I harp each day Thy praise,
O Giver of Life,
and may I each day give love to Thee,
Green Spirit.
Each night may I do the same;
each day and night, dark and light,
may I sense Thy Presence with me
in quiet moments in my garden,
and may I carry Thee with me
as I go forth into my life.

O most honored Greening Force,
You who roots in the Sun;
You who lights up, in shining serenity,
within a wheel
that earthly excellence fails to comprehend.
You are enfolded
in the weaving of divine mysteries.

— **HILDEGARD VON BINGEN**

The kiss of the sun for pardon,
The song of the birds for mirth,
One is nearer God's heart in a garden
Than anywhere else on earth.

— **DOROTHY FRANCES GURNEY**

God is the experience of looking at a tree
and saying, "Ah!"

—JOSEPH CAMPBELL

As the earth gives birth to her sprouts,
and as a garden causes
what is sown in her to spring up,
so the Life-Giver will cause
justice and song to branch forth
before all people.

—ISAIAH 61:11

> I come in the little things,
> Saith the Lord:
> ... I have set My Feet
> Amidst the delicate and bladed wheat
> That spring triumphant in the furrowed sod.
> There so I dwell, in weakness and in power;
> Not broken or divided, saith our God!
> In your strait garden plot I come to flower:
> About your porch My Vine
> Meek, fruitful, doth entwine;
> Waits, at the threshold, Love's appointed hour.

—**EVELYN UNDERHILL**

Study Nature as the countenance of God.

—**CHARLES KINGSLEY**

Some keep the Sabbath going to Church,
I keep it staying at Home—
With a bobolink for a Chorister,
And an Orchard, for a Dome.

—EMILY DICKINSON

Connection with gardens,
even small ones,
even potted plants,
can become windows to the inner life.
The simple act of stopping
and looking at the beauty around us
can be prayer.

—PATRICIA R. BARRETT

I ask the Great Creator silently, daily, and often many times a day, to permit me to speak to God through the three great Kingdoms of the world which He has created—the animal, mineral, and vegetable Kingdoms—to understand their relations to each other, and our relations to them and to the Great God who made all of us. I ask God daily and often momently to give me wisdom, understanding, and bodily strength to do God's will; hence I am asking and receiving all the time.

—GEORGE WASHINGTON CARVER

If you love the Dharma, you have to farm it. Go to a garden. Just stand in it. Breathe in the air, the fragrances, the light, the temperature, the music of the different plants, insects, birds, worms, caterpillars, grasshoppers, and butterflies. Inhale the prana (cosmic energy) of all the abundantly growing things. Recharge your inner batteries. This is the joy of natural meditation.

—LAMA SURYA DAS

I love to think of nature
as an unlimited broadcasting station,
through which God speaks to us every hour,
if we will only tune in.

—GEORGE WASHINGTON CARVER

The realm of heaven is like a mustard seed,
which a person took and planted in a field.
It starts out smaller than any of the other
seeds—but when it is full grown, it is larger
than all the other plants in the garden, as tall
as a tree, so that the winged ones of heaven
come and dwell in its branches.

—JESUS

11

WE ARE THE GARDEN

O heavenly Sower,
plough me first,
and then cast
the truth into me,
and let me yield thee
a bounteous harvest.

—CHARLES SPURGEON

Christ's rich garden ever upward towers.
For Christ sweet showers of Grace
makes on it fall.

—EDWARD TAYLOR

Cultivate your whole being,
As you would cultivate a garden
—with attention, care, and even love.

—KEN COHEN

I will water my heart
in the nine rays of the sun.
Love be my fertilizer,
helping me to grow.
Benevolence be in my mind,
pulling out the weeds of malice.
I am the white rose;
my scent is a blessing to all.
I will grow in the power of the Life-Giver,
in the likeness of fertile soil,
in the likeness of sprouting seed,
in the likeness of fruitful vine,
and in the likeness of all things green.
Love be my fertilizer,
helping me to grow.

What a secret thing the sap is! The roots go searching through the soil with their little spongioles, but we cannot see them suck out the various gases, or transmute the mineral into the vegetable; this work is done down in the dark. Our root is Christ Jesus, and our life is hid in him; this is the secret of the Lord. The radix of the Christian life is as secret as the life itself. How permanently active is the sap in the cedar! In the Christian the divine life is always full of energy—not always in fruit-bearing, but in inward operations.

The believer's graces, are not every one of them in constant motion? but their lives never cease to palpitate within. They are not always working for God, but their hearts are always living upon God. As the sap manifests itself in producing the foliage and fruit of the tree, so with truly healthy Christians. . . . If you notice their actions you will see that they have been with Jesus. They have so much sap within, that it must fill their conduct and conversation with life.

—**CHARLES SPURGEON**

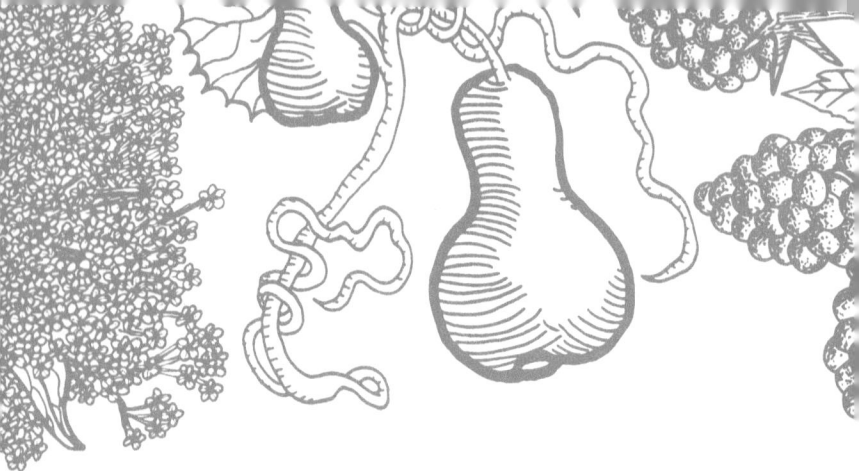

Cultivate a thankful spirit!
It will be to you a perpetual feast.

—JOHN R. MACDUFF

Be like a tree planted firmly
by springs of water,
yielding your fruit in season.
Your leaf will not wither,
and you will go forward in all you do.

—PSALM 1:3

Who would have thought my shriveled heart
Could have recovered greenness? It was gone
Quite underground; as flowers depart. . . .
And now in age I bud again.

—GEORGE HERBERT

I am the vine, you are the branches.
If you remain in Me and I in you,
then you will bear much fruit.
Apart from Me, you would have
no power to bring forth life.

—JESUS

Spirit, plant in me Thy wisdom.
Spirit, prune me with Thy justice.
Spirit, water me with Thy mercy.
Spirit, warm me with Thy sunshine.
Spirit, make me bountiful with Thy fullness.
Spirit, shield me with Thy shade.
Spirit, fill me with Thy grace,
for Thou art the seed
that grows in me,
Thou are the Spirit of the Garden
that lives in me.

This is indeed well understood by any gardener. The aim of the life of a rosebush is to be all that is inherent as potentiality in the rosebush: . . . The goal of living is to grow optimally according to the conditions of human existence and thus to become fully what one potentially is.

—ERICH FROMM

ABOUT THE SOURCES

Prince Albert (1819–1861) The husband of Queen Victoria, both he and the Queen were avid gardeners who planted hundreds of trees, a vegetable and fruit garden, and flower beds. He encouraged their children to learn about growing food in their own little garden, and he even bought the produce from them at market rates.

A. Bronson Alcott (1799–1888) The father of the author Louisa May Alcott, he was also an educator and abolitionist. He founded the Fruitlands commune, which was a vegetarian farming community that used no animal labor.

Henri Frédéric Amiel (1821–1881) A Swiss philosopher and poet.

Alfred Austin (1835–1913) An English poet who wrote about Nature and gardens.

Emilie Barnes (1938–2016) An inspirational women's author.

Patricia R. Barrett An Episcopal priest, gardener, and the author of several books on gardening.

J. M. Barrie (1860–1937) The author of *Peter Pan*, he also wrote stories about a baby boy who has magical adventures in Kensington Gardens in London.

H. E. Bates (1905–1974) A novelist and short story writer, he became known for his writing about the countryside and the life of the agricultural laborer.

John Berger (1926–2017) An English novelist, painter, and poet.

Wendell Berry (1934–) Poet, essayist, activist, and farmer who writes about farming, the land, and sustainable agriculture.

Henry Beston (1888–1968) An American writer and naturalist who helped inspire the modern environmental movement.

Hildegard von Bingen (1098–1179) A German mystic, writer, composer, herbologist, and artist, she wrote about "viriditas," the "green force" that fills the world.

William Blake (1757–1827) An English artist, poet, and visionary.

Jacob Boehme (1575–1624) German mystic and theologian.

Barbara Dodge Borland (1904–1991) American author who wrote *This Is the Way My Garden Grows*.

Hal Borland (1900–1978) The husband of Barbara Dodge Borland, he was an American author and naturalist who wrote many books about the outdoors.

Robert Brault American writer.

Richard Briers (1934–2013) British actor.

Jacob Bronowski (1908–1974) British mathematician and historian who developed a humanistic approach to science.

T. E. Brown (1830–1897) Scholar, poet, and theologian from the Isle of Man.

The Buddha (fifth–fourth centuries BCE) The Awakened One, founder of Buddhism

Luther Burbank (1849–1926) American botanist, horticulturist, and pioneer in agricultural science.

Robert Burns (1759–1796) Scottish poet.

Joseph Campbell (1904–1987) American professor of literature who developed a theory of comparative mythology and religion.

Thomas Carlyle (1795–1881) British historian, essayist, and philosopher.

Jim Carrey (1962–) Canadian-American actor, comedian, and producer.

George Washington Carver (1860s–1943) An American agricultural scientist and inventor, he promoted methods to prevent soil depletion; he was the most prominent black scientist of the early twentieth century.

Willa Cather (1873–1947) American author who wrote about frontier life on the Great Plains.

G. K. Chesterton (1874–1936) English author and theologian.

Cicero (106–43 BCE) Roman statesman and philosopher.

Ken Cohen (1952–) A world-renowned qigong and tai chi master, he is a leader in the dialogue between ancient Asian wisdom and modern science.

Joseph S. Cotter Sr. (1861–1949) Poet, playwright, and community leader, he was one of the first black American playwrights to be published.

Jeff Cox (1940–) An editor of *Organic Gardening* throughout the 1970s, he is also the author of seventeen books and countless magazine articles about organic produce and gardening.

Thalassa Cruso (1909–1997) British-born author and television presenter on horticulture.

Charles Dickens (1812–1870) English author and social critic.

Emily Dickinson (1830–1886) American poet who once said, "I was reared in the garden"; a recluse who perhaps had agoraphobia, her garden was one of the few things that drew her out of the house.

Benjamin Disraeli (1804–1881) British politician who served as the prime minister of the United Kingdom. He also wrote novels.

Ursula Elliott (1944–) An amateur gardener and avid letter writer.

Ralph Waldo Emerson (1803–1882) American essayist, lecturer, philosopher, and poet who led the transcendentalist movement. He believed in the interconnectedness of Nature and all things.

Ruth Shaw Ernst (1918–2009) The author of *The Naturalist's Garden*.

John Erskine (1879–1951) American educator, author, composer, and pianist.

John Evelyn (1620–1706) English writer and gardener.

Reginald Farrer (1880–1920) English traveler and plant collector who published a number of books, although he is best known for *My Rock Garden*. He traveled to Asia in search of a variety of plants, many of which he brought back to England.

Rachel Field (1894–1942) American novelist, poet, and children's author.

H. L. V. Fletcher (1902–1974) English author of many books on gardening.

Erich Fromm (1900–1980) Psychoanalyst and philosopher who fled the Nazi regime and settled in the United States.

Robert Frost (1874–1963) American poet who wrote about rural life.

Thomas Fuller (1608–1661) English scholar, preacher, and author.

Mahatma Gandhi (1869–1948) An Indian lawyer and activist who used nonviolent resistance to lead the successful campaign for India's independence. His philosophy continues to inspire movements for civil rights and freedom across the world.

Michael P. Garafalo Poet and author of *Greenway Research* website.

John Gerard (1545–1612) English botanist who was the author of a 1,484-page illustrated *Herball*, or *Generall Historie of Plantes*, first published in 1597, which became the most popular botany book in English in the seventeenth century.

Johann Wolfgang von Goethe (1749–1832) A German novelist and poet who was also particularly interested in botany.

Elizabeth Goudge (1900–1984) English novelist who wrote about the beauties and spiritual meaning of the English countryside.

Anne Chotzinoff Grossman (1930–2002) An author and translator of operas.

C. Z. Guest (1920–2003) An American stage actress, author, columnist, horsewoman, fashion designer, and socialite who was known as a fashion icon.

Dorothy Frances Gurney (1858–1932) English poet and hymn writer.

Nathaniel Hawthorne (1804–1864) American novelist and short story writer.

William Hazlitt (1778–1830) An English essayist, drama and literary critic, painter, social commentator, and philosopher.

George Herbert (1593–1633) English priest and devotional poet.

Gerard Manley Hopkins (1844–1889) English poet and Jesuit priest who praised God with vivid Nature imagery.

Thomas Jefferson (1743–1826) American politician and philosopher, he was also an avid gardener whose garden contained 330 varieties of 89 species of vegetables and herbs, and 170 varieties of the finest fruit varieties known at the time. He was known for constantly handing out seeds to friends and acquaintances.

Gertrude Jekyll (1843–1942) A British horticulturist, garden designer, craftswoman, photographer, writer, and artist, she created over four hundred gardens in the United Kingdom, Europe, and the United States, and wrote more than a thousand articles for gardening magazines.

Jesus (c. 4 BCE–c. 30 CE) A first-century Jewish preacher, who is the central figure of Christianity and is seen as the incarnation of God. He frequently taught using parables and metaphors from farming

Jamie Jobb An American writer.

Lyndon B. Johnson (1908–1973) American president. His wife Lady Bird was known for her environmental work; she brought her flower garden inside for everything from state events to social gatherings.

Charles Kingsley (1819–1875) A priest of the Church of England, he was also a university professor, social reformer, historian, novelist, and poet. His interest in natural science led him to a friendship with Charles Darwin.

Rudyard Kipling (1865–1936) English author who was born in India, and was inspired by India's natural world. As an adult, he settled in England, where he spent hours planning his garden; when he won the Nobel Prize for Literature, he spent all the prize-money on his garden.

Jack Kramer (1927–). Author of many gardening books.

Charles Lamb (1775–1834) English essayist and poet.

William Lawson (1554–1634) English cleric who wrote books on gardening.

Anne Morrow Lindbergh (1906–2001) American author (also the wife of aviator Charles Lindbergh), she wrote *Gifts from the Sea*, which some people see as being a forerunner of the Green Movement.

Sheryl London Author of books on food gardening.

James Russell Lowell (1819–1891) American poet.

John R. MacDuff (1818–1895) Scottish minister and the author of religious essays.

Andrew Marvel (1621–1678) English poet.

Julie Moir Messervy Award-winning landscape architect.

Joaquin Miller (1837–1913) American poet and frontiersman who wrote about the beauties of the Sierra Mountains.

Claude Monet (1840–1926) French Impressionist painter famous for his paintings of gardens and Nature.

Beverley Nichols (1898–1983) English author who wrote gardening classics.

JoAnna O'Keefe Poet who wrote *Come to the Garden*.

Georgia O'Keeffe (1887–1986) American artist known for her paintings of enlarged flowers.

Mirabel Osler (1925–2016) An English writer and garden designer. Her book *A Gentle Plea for Chaos*, based on her experiences in her garden in Shropshire, was said by the *New York Times* to send "a blast of fresh air through the stuffy rooms of the English gardening world when it was first published."

Russell Page (1906–1985) A British gardener and landscape architect.

George Peele (1556–1599) English poet and dramatist.

Eleanor Perenyi (1918–2009) American gardener and author.

J. M. Price (1857–1924) An artist, war correspondent, explorer, journalist, and caricaturist for *Vanity Fair*.

Rainer Maria Rilke (1875–1926) Austrian poet whose works have been widely translated.

Hanna Rion (1875–1924) An American-born author and translator (who later lived in England), she was also an avid gardener.

John Ruskin (1819–1900) English art critic, philosopher, and social critic.

V. Sackville-West (1892–1962) English author and garden designer.

Edna St. Vincent Millay (1892–1950) An American poet, she frequently used images drawn from nature in her work; she loved plants and devoted time every day to working in her gardens.

May Sarton (1912–1995) American poet and novelist who wrote at length about her garden in her journals.

John Seymour (1914–2004) Sometimes called the father of the self-sufficiency movement, he was a writer, broadcaster, environmentalist, farmer, and activist.

William Shakespeare (1564–1616) English poet and playwright; 175 different plants are mentioned in his works.

George Bernard Shaw (1856–1950) Irish playwright and political activist; many of his plays were written in his garden.

Isaac Bashevis Singer (1902–1991) Polish-American author.

George Sitwell (1860–1943) British antiquarian, politician, and gardener.

Christopher Smart (1722–1771) English poet; one of his long poems is on how to garden hops.

Charles Spurgeon (1834–1892) English preacher.

Ruth Stout (1884–1980) An American author best known for her "No Work" gardening books and techniques.

Fred Streeter (1879–1975) British horticulturalist.

Dr. SunWolf University professor, author, lawyer, folklorist.

Lama Surya Das (1950–) An American lama in the Tibetan Buddhist tradition. He is a poet, spiritual activist, author of many popular works on Buddhism, meditation teacher, and spokesperson for Buddhism in the West.

Edward Taylor (1642–1729) Colonial American poet.

Henry David Thoreau (1817–1862) American essayist and philosopher who recommended a simple life lived close to Nature.

C. E. Thorne Late nineteenth-century agriculturalist.

Alice B. Toklas (1877–1967) An American-born member of the Parisian avant-garde of the early twentieth century, she was the life partner of American writer Gertrude Stein; she wrote her memoir in the form of a cookbook.

Evelyn Underhill (1875–1942) English author known for her work on religion and spiritual practice, especially mysticism.

Abram L. Urban Twentieth-century author who wrote about his garden.

Charles Dudley Warner (1829–1900) American essayist and novelist.

Beth Weidner Twenty-first-century writer.

Opal Whiteley (1897–1992) American nature writer and diarist.

Walt Whitman (1819–1892) American poet, essayist, and journalist.

Barbara Winkler Twenty-first-century physician.

William Wordsworth (1770–1850) English poet whose work focused on the role of Nature.

Celtic Nature Prayers
Prayers from an Ancient Well

Find God in Nature
Pray for Our Endangered Planet

Long before they had heard about Christianity, the Celts knew that Nature was their portal to a great spiritual reality. Wells, mountain crags, caves, and lochs were "thin places" that allowed access to the realm of spirits. In these temples of Nature, the Celts sought physical and spiritual healing, as well as revelation. The salmon, the eagle, and even the tiny hazelnut, all were allies in helping humanity access the mysterious magic that underlay physical matter.

**Paperback Price:
$14.95**

**Kindle Price:
$5.99**

Water from an Ancient Well

Celtic Spirituality for Modern Life

A Fresh Look at Celtic Spirituality

Using story, scripture, reflection, and prayer, this book offers readers a taste of the living water that refreshed the ancient Celts. The author invites readers to imitate the Celtic saints who were aware of God as a living presence in everybody and everything. This ancient perspective gives radical new alternatives to modern faith practices, ones that are both challenging and constructively positive. This is a Christianity big enough to embrace the entire world.

Paperback Price: $19.99

Kindle Price: $7.49

Forest Church
A Field Guide to a Spiritual Connection with Nature

Brimming with insights and packed with information, this book draws you out, quite literally, into Nature to experience a new, well-thought-through pattern of spiritual practice. Bruce Stanley gives you all the resources you'll need, both practical and theoretical, to get going with a group or on your own.

Forest Church is a fresh expression of church drawing on much older traditions when sacred places and practices were outside—but it is also drawing on contemporary research that highlights the benefits of spending time with Nature in wild places.

Paperback Price: $14.75

Kindle Price: $5.99

The Soul of the Green Man

The Green Man is an ancient symbol that has gained new popularity, and yet his origins and meaning remain a mystery. Kenneth McIntosh, author of *Water from an Ancient Well: Celtic Spirituality for Modern Life,* offers a seldom-heard theory on the original significance of this leafy visage. With a wealth of color photographs and drawings, the author traces the Green Man's family tree, revealing the deep spirituality embedded in this archetypal image, and concludes with the hope the Green Man offers us today in the twenty-first century.

Celtic shamanic healer Lilly Weichberger says, "For anyone with a love of Celtic history, nature, and spirituality, whether it be Christian or Pagan, this book is a must-read!"

Paperback Price: $29.99

Kindle Price: $9.99

Sacred Soil

A Gardener's Book of Reflection

In these fifteen intimate essays, Melina Rudman explores the pain of loss and the joy of connection, all within the context of her garden. She writes of gardening as a spiritual practice, one that has the power to ground us in the seasons and cycles of Nature. Gardening, she says, plants us firmly in the circle of birth, life, and death, "smack dab in the middle of life's gore and glory." While gardening focuses on the world of touch and sight and scent, it also opens doors to deeper realities. It teaches us resilience; it shows us how to let go; it comforts our aching hearts; it leads us to repentance—and it offers us a conduit to the Divine.

Paperback Price: $12.99

Kindle Price: $6.99

Anamchara Books

www.AnamcharaBooks.com

www.ingramcontent.com/pod-product-compliance
Lightning Source LLC
Chambersburg PA
CBHW060526080526
44586CB00012B/639